Trace each number. Use this page as a reference.

0 1 2 3 4

5 6 7 8

9 10 11 12

13 14 15 16

17 18 19 20

Trace and write the number and number word.

0 0 0 0 0

0

zero

zero

Color the picture.

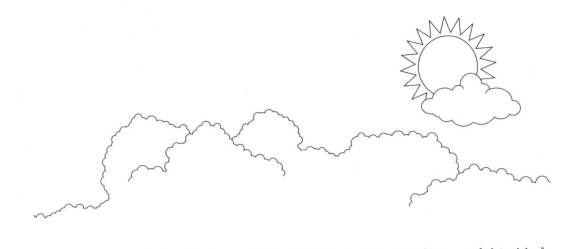

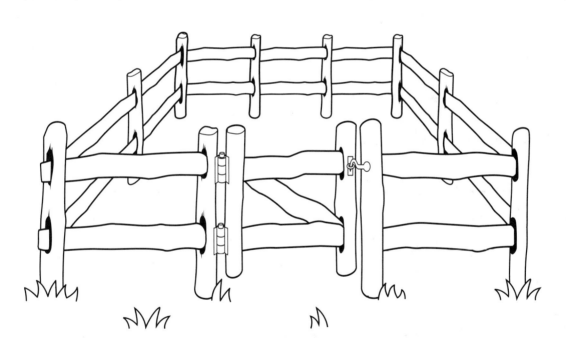

0 animals

Trace and write the number and number word.

1

one

Color the picture.

1 barn

Trace and write the number and number word.

2 2 2 2 2

2

two

two

Color the picture.

2 farmers

Trace and write the number and number word.

3 3 3 3 3

3

three

three

Color the picture.

3 scarecrows

Trace and write the number and number word.

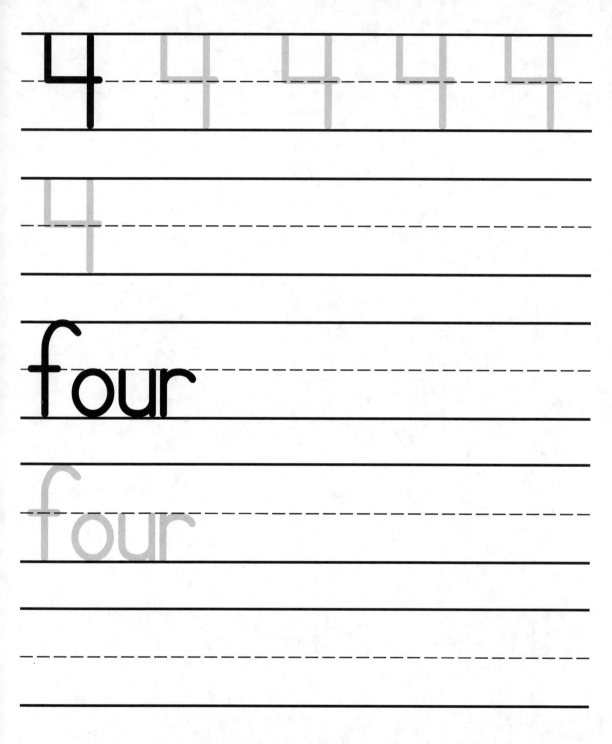

Color the picture.

4 horses

Trace and write the number and number word.

5 5 5 5 5

5

five

five

Color the picture.

5 cows

Trace and write the number and number word.

6 6 6 6 6

6

six

six

Color the picture.

6 fish

Trace and write the number and number word.

7 7 7 7 7

7

seven

seven

Color the picture.

7 cats

Trace and write the number and number word.

8 8 8 8 8

8

eight

eight

Color the picture.

8 dogs

Trace and write the number and number word.

9 9 9 9 9

9

nine

nine

Color the picture.

q sheep

Trace and write the number and number word.

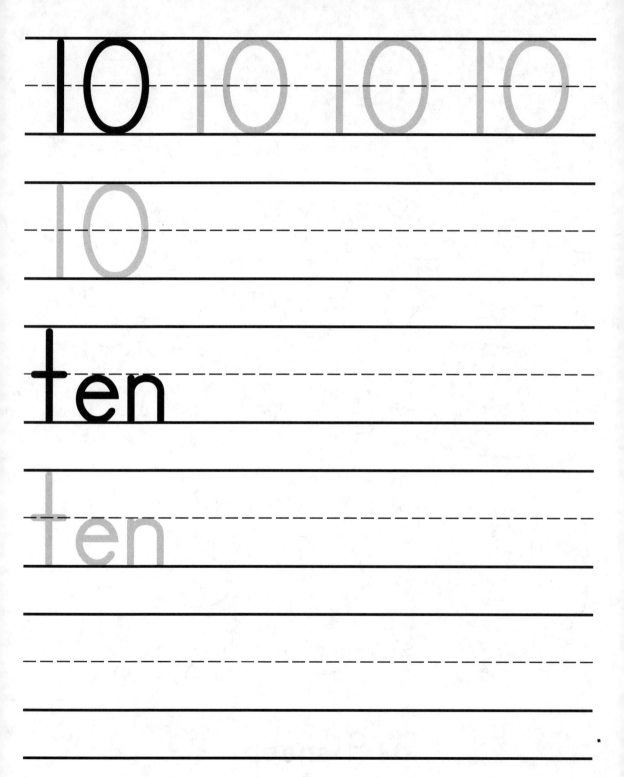

10 10 10 10 10

10

ten

ten

Color the picture.

10 ducks

Trace and write the number and number word.

11

eleven

eleven

Color the picture.

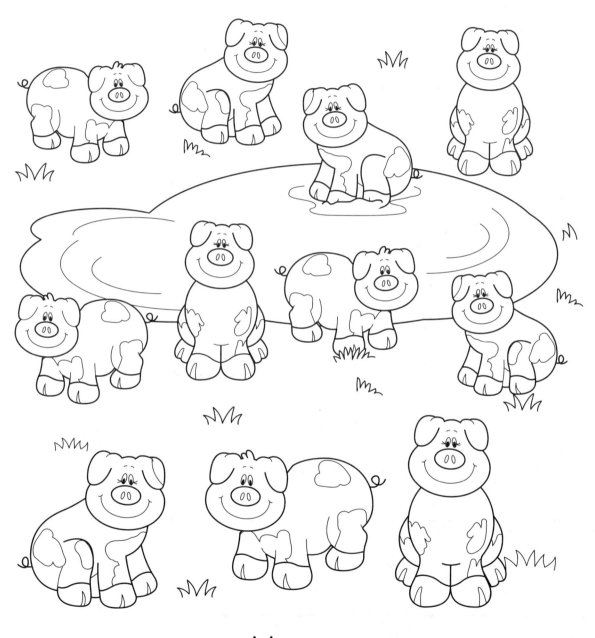

11 pigs

Trace and write the number and number word.

12 12 12 12 12

12

twelve

twelve

Color the picture.

12 sunflowers

Trace and write the number and number word.

13 13 13 13

13

thirteen

thirteen

Color the picture.

13 cornstalks

Trace and write the number and number word.

14 14 14 14 14

14

fourteen

fourteen

Color the picture.

14 watermelons

Trace and write the number and number word.

15 15 15 15

15

fifteen

fifteen

Color the picture.

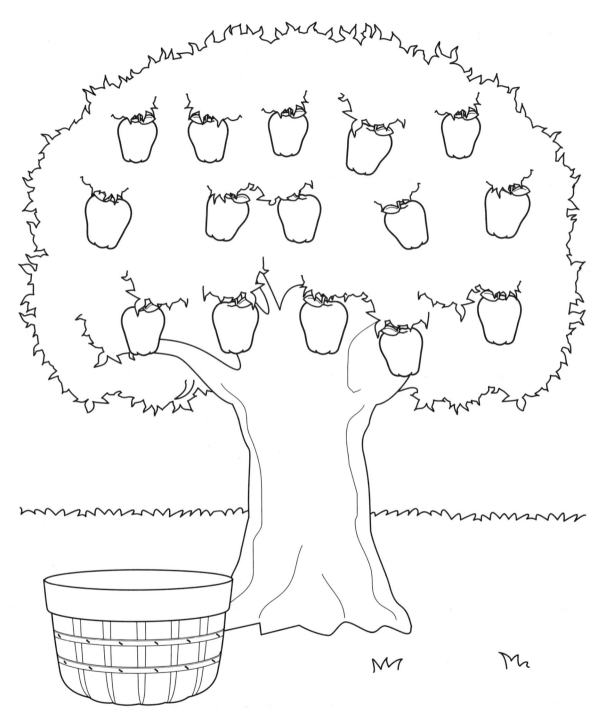

15 apples

Trace and write the number and number word.

sixteen

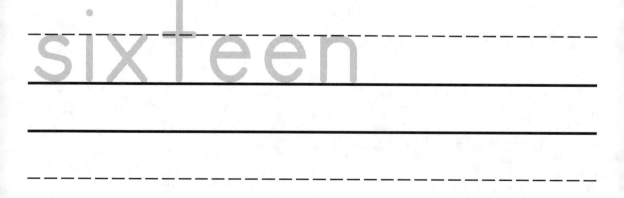

Color the picture.

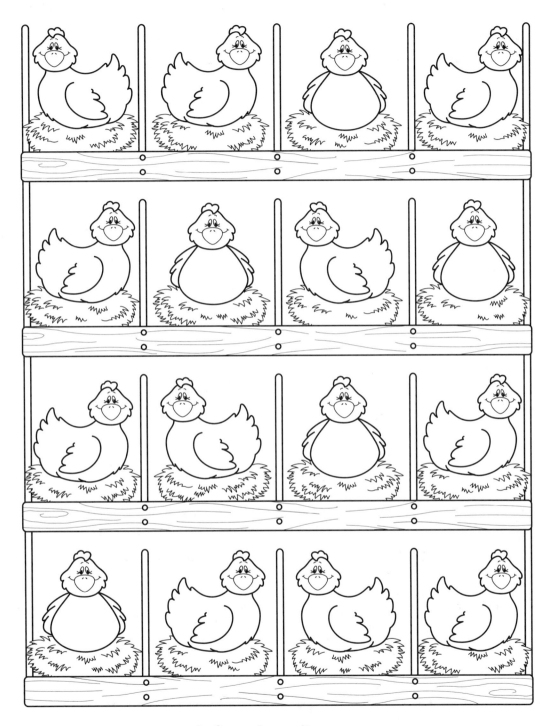

16 chickens

Trace and write the number and number word.

17   17   17   17

17

seventeen

seventeen

Color the picture.

17 mice

Trace and write the number and number word.

18   18   18

18

eighteen

eighteen

Color the picture.

18 hay bales

Trace and write the number and number word.

19 19 19 19 19

19 19

nineteen

nineteen

Color the picture.

19 crows

Trace and write the number and number word.

20   20   20   20

20

twenty

twenty

Color the picture.

20 bees

Count the items in each box. Circle the correct number.

5   2   4

3   0   1

1   5   0

2   3   4

Count the items in each box. Circle the correct number.

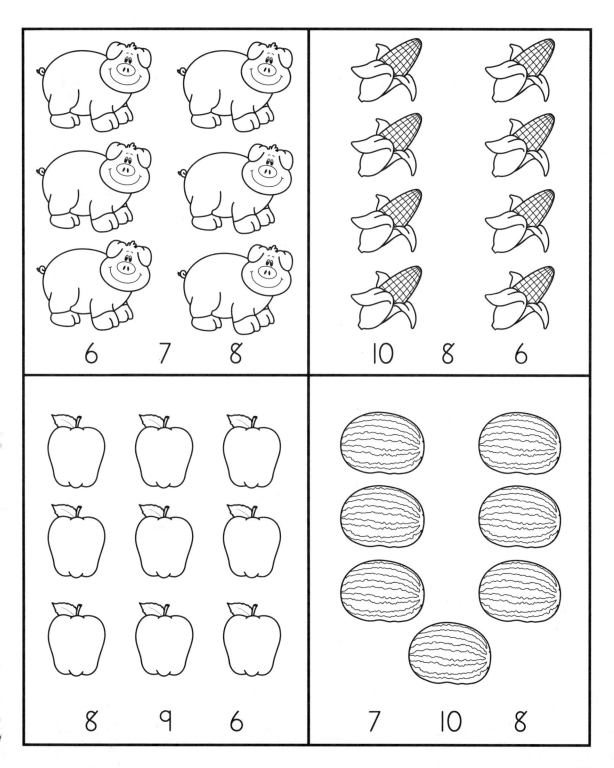

6   7   8

10   8   6

8   9   6

7   10   8

Count the items in each box. Circle the correct number.

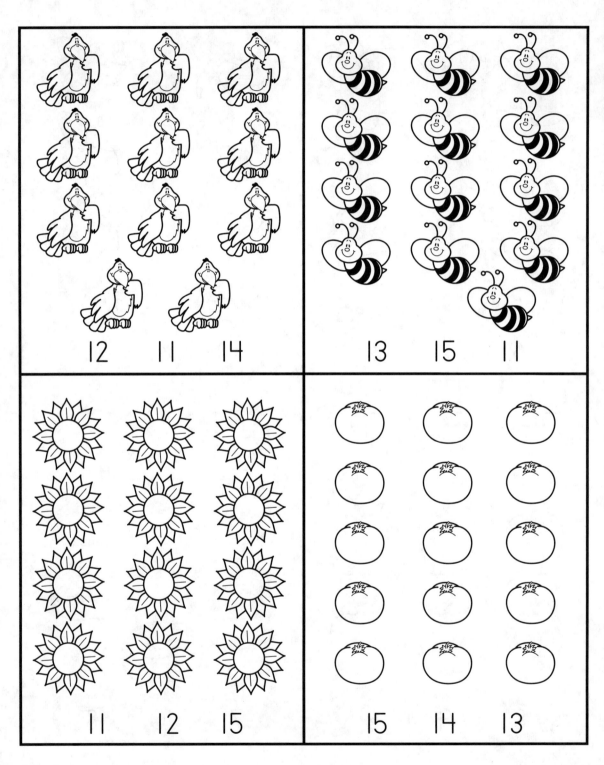

12   11   14

13   15   11

11   12   15

15   14   13

Count the items in each box. Circle the correct number.

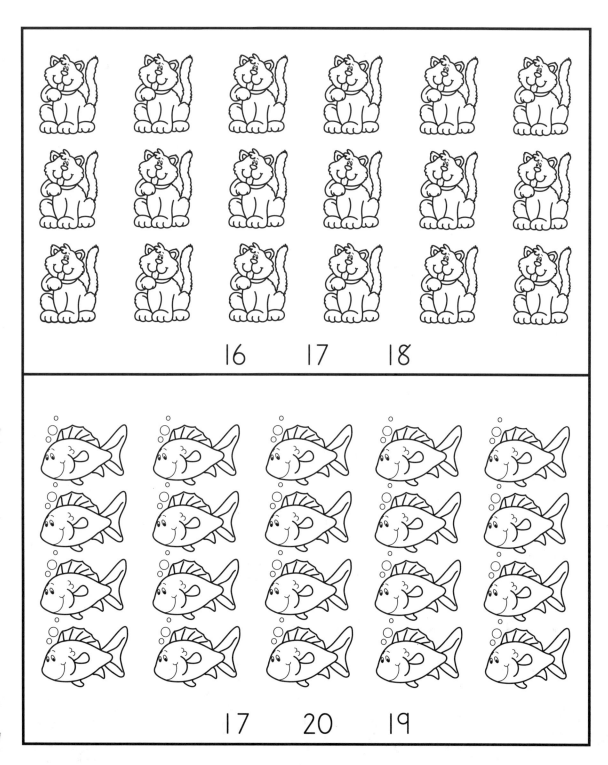

16   17   18

17   20   19

Count the items in each box. Circle the correct number.

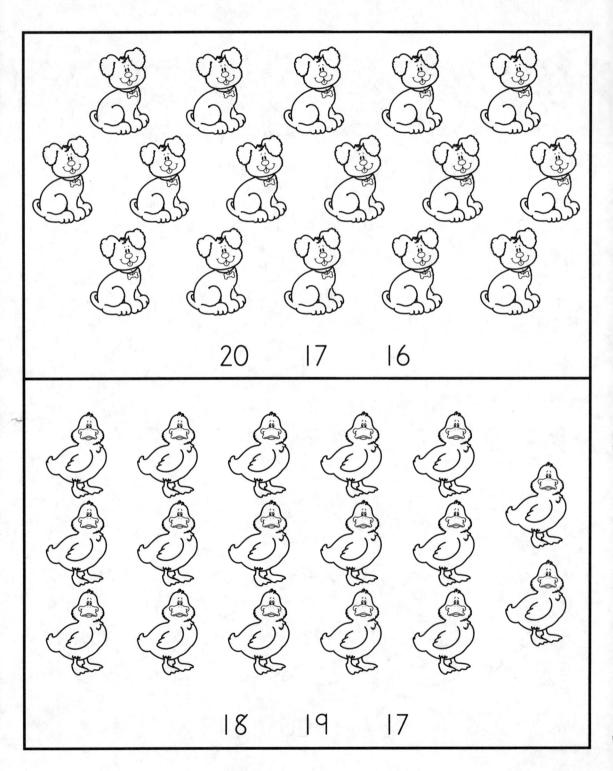

20   17   16

18   19   17

Color the correct number of items to match the number shown.

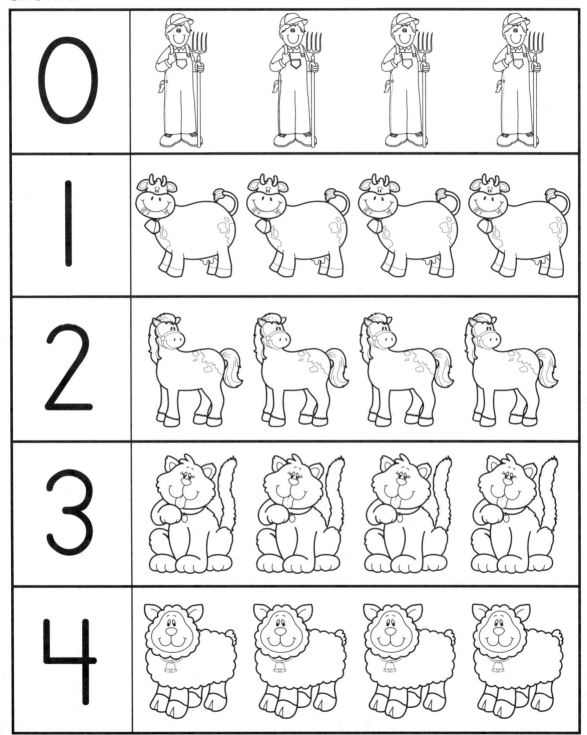

Color the correct number of items to match the number shown.

5	
6	
7	
8	

Color the correct number of items to match the number shown.

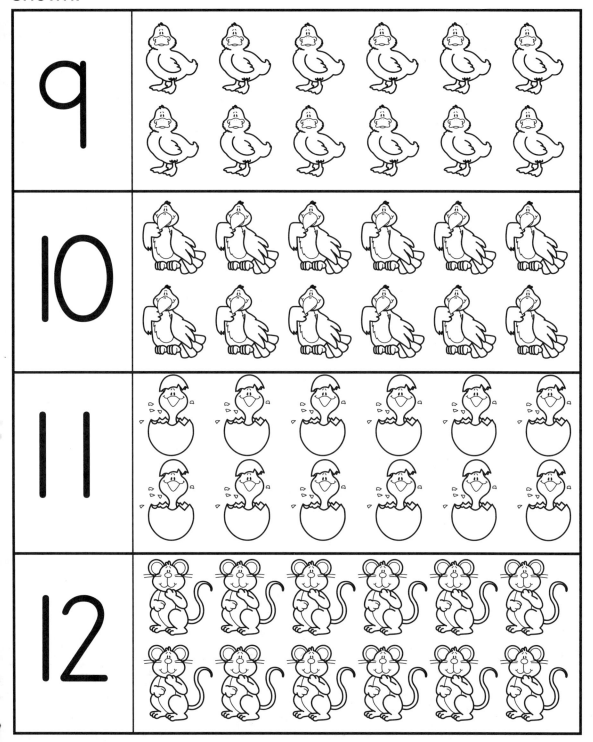

Color the correct number of items to match the number shown.

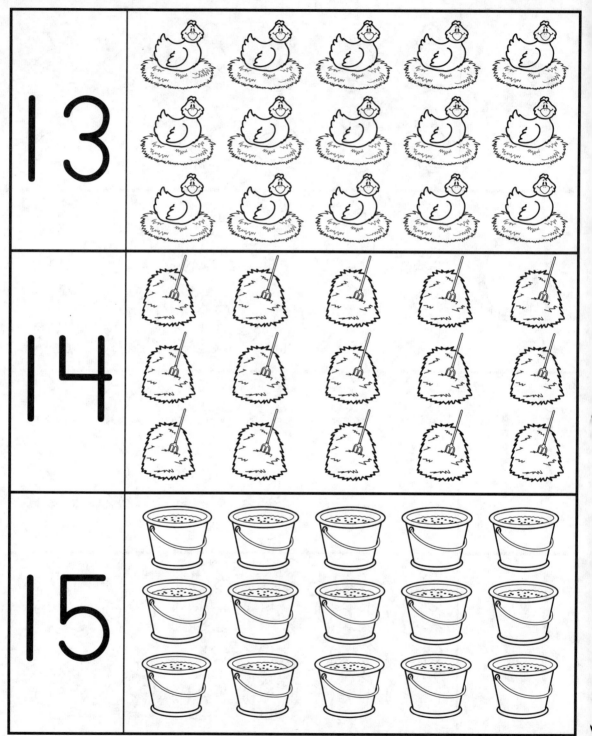

Color the correct number of items to match the number shown.

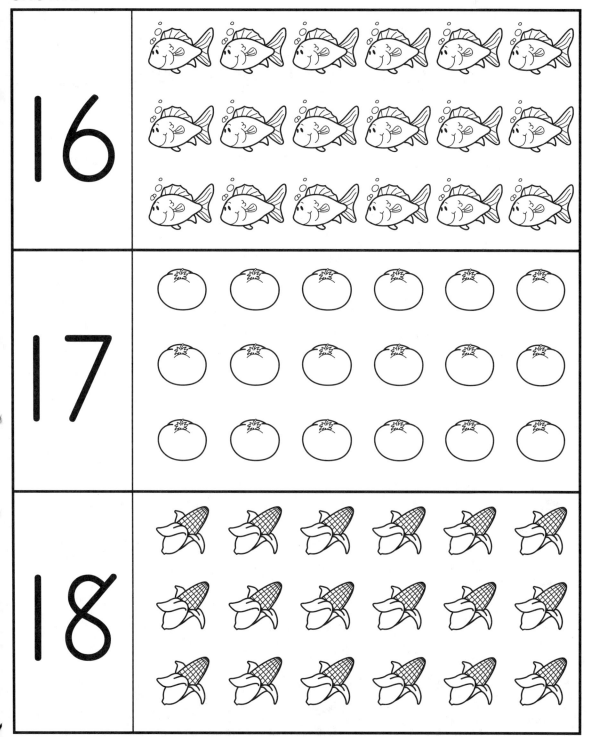

Color the correct number of items to match the number shown.

19

20

Color: 0–red   2–yellow   4–blue   6–black
       1–orange 3–green   5–brown

Color: 7–black   9–blue   11–orange   13–green
8–brown   10–red   12–yellow

Color: 14–orange 16–red 18–brown 20–blue
15–green 17–black 19–yellow

Draw lines to connect the numbers to their correct number words.

6   six

3   two

0   four

4   three

1   zero

5   one

2   five

Draw lines to connect the numbers to their correct number words.

7	nine
11	thirteen
13	eight
12	twelve
9	seven
8	ten
10	eleven

Draw lines to connect the numbers to their correct number words.

19	fifteen
16	nineteen
14	eighteen
17	twenty
18	seventeen
15	sixteen
20	fourteen

Color: zero–black   two–yellow   four–blue
one–orange   three–green

Color: five—blue   seven—green   nine—brown
        six—yellow   eight—orange

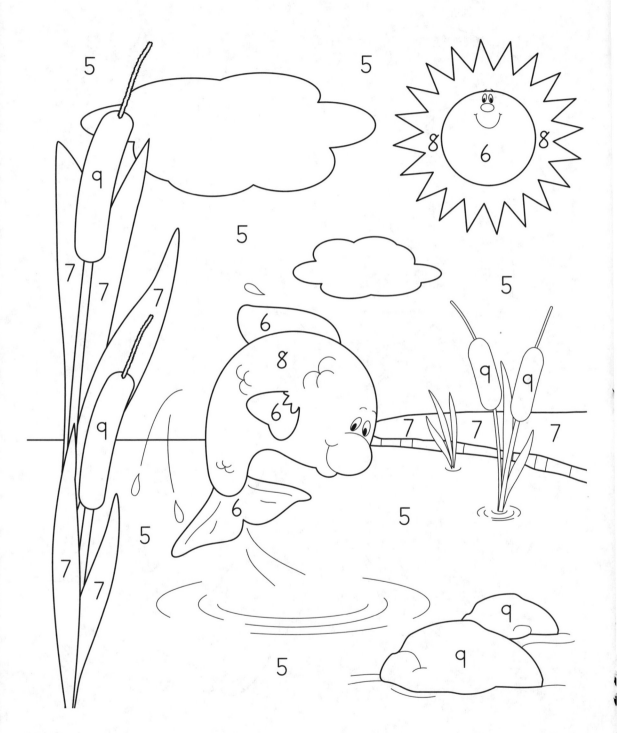

Color: ten—green   twelve—orange   fourteen—black
eleven—blue   thirteen—yellow

Color: fifteen–yellow seventeen–blue nineteen–orange
sixteen–green eighteen–red   twenty–brown